USING SHAPE

This book belongs to

_____

_____

Rose Griffiths

Illustrated by David Farris

Notes for parents

The activities in this book have been written for children aged 5 to 7, who are working on Key Stage 1 of the National Curriculum at school.

'Shape' is not just about triangles, squares and other geometrical forms. The National Curriculum's work on 'Shape and Space' includes looking for patterns, describing where things are, and showing how things can be moved, as well as sorting, identifying and using shapes. And remember that most of the shapes around us are not simple ones!

Many of the activities in this book can be followed up with similar common-sense ideas at home. Encourage your child to be observant, and to look for similarities and differences between things. Drawing things from real life is a very useful activity, especially if you suggest particular things for your child to concentrate on (for example, 'Can you copy the pattern on my jumper?').

Painting, printing and colouring patterns, doing jigsaws, and using beads, buttons or food (when cooking) to make patterns and shapes in two dimensions are also useful.

Working in three dimensions is equally important, even though it is difficult to do so in a two-dimensional workbook! Try to provide your child with as much time as possible to build and play with construction toys, building bricks, and boxes and cartons. Provide people, cars and animals to make things for, and encourage your child to explain what she or he is doing.

Children naturally vary a great deal in their achievements in maths, so don't feel you must push your child to complete every activity in this book straight away. Remember that people of all ages usually learn best if they enjoy what they are doing, and if they do not try to learn too much in one go!

This edition first published 1991 by Hodder and Stoughton Educational,
a division of Hodder and Stoughton Ltd, Mill Road, Dunton Green, Sevenoaks, Kent

ISBN 0 340 55072 4

Designed and typeset by DP Press Ltd, Sevenoaks, Kent

Printed by Colorcraft, Hong Kong

Mouse hunt

My pet mice have escaped. Help me look for them!

Did you find these mice? ✓ or ✗

The mouse under the chair. ☐

The mouse behind the clock. ☐

The mouse next to the books. ☐

The mouse on the table. ☐

The mouse in the bag. ☐

Buttons

I need 3 more buttons like this to go on my coat. Can you find my buttons for me?

Can you find any other sets of buttons? You can colour them in if you want to.

4

Patterns

I've drawn some patterns. Draw what comes next!

My scarf has a pattern. The stripes are red, then blue, then yellow.

Colour my scarf for me!

Left

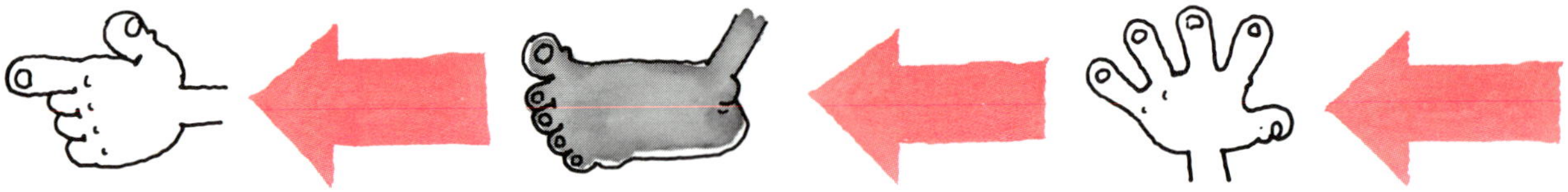

I'm waving with my left hand.

Are we all waving with our left hands?

Put 'Yes' or 'No'.

_____   _____   _____   _____

6

Right

I'm holding balloons in my right hand.

I don't like balloons. I'm going right out of the way!

Are we all holding balloons in our right hands?

Put 'Yes' or 'No'.

Fences

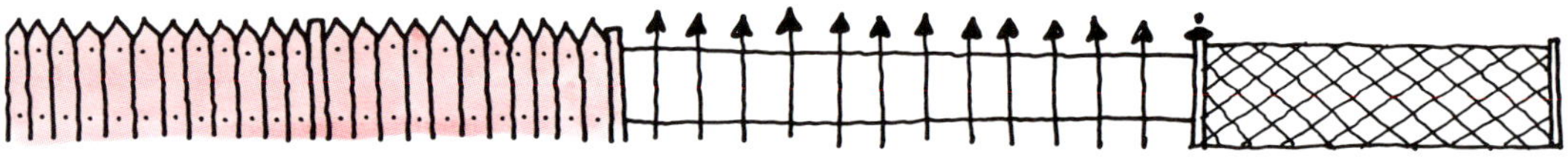

We've been looking at fences.

They are made in lots of different patterns.

Draw the rest of each fence. Keep to the same pattern.

This fence is tall, to keep footballs in the playground.

This fence is short, so we can see the flowers.

Look at the fences near where you live.
Look at the patterns they are made in.
Try to draw some of them!

Shape names

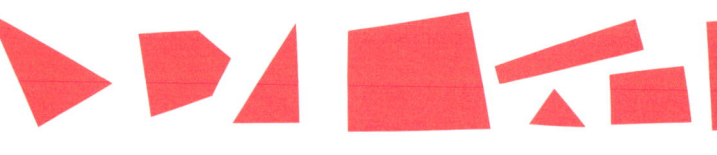

I want to learn the names of some shapes.

We'll help you!

We'll tell you the names of some shapes with straight sides.

Triangles have 3 straight sides.
These are all triangles:

Are these shapes all triangles?
Write 'Yes' or 'No' for each one.

———————   ———————   ———————   ———————

Rectangles have 4 straight sides.

These are all rectangles: But these are not:

Are these shapes all rectangles?
Write 'Yes' or 'No' for each one.

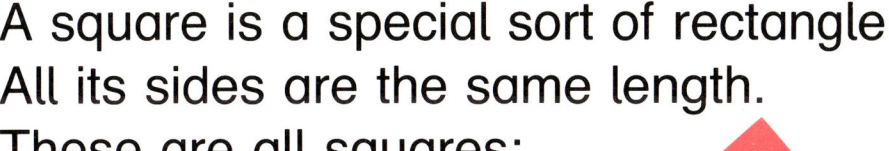

_____   _____   _____   _____

A square is a special sort of rectangle.
All its sides are the same length.
These are all squares:

Are these shapes all squares?
Write 'Yes' or 'No' for each one.

_____   _____   _____   _____

Brick maze

I made a maze with bricks, for my little person to walk in.

Can you draw a path to the castle?
Can you draw a path to the mountain?

WAY IN

Could you build a maze with bricks?
It's not easy!
Could you build a castle or a mountain?

Circles

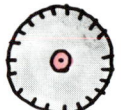   

We're looking at circles!

Can you tell what the things on this page are? They all have circles on them.

Which picture is which?

plug hole   mug   clock   can of drink

_____

_____

_____

_____

Have you got a bicycle?

Find a bike to look at.
How many circles can you
find on it?

_____

Could you ride a bike
with square wheels?

_____

Umbrellas

Colour our umbrellas.
Make each one different.

16

Sunglasses

Salad

I made a salad with these:

cabbage

celery

carrot

cheese

Draw lines to show which things these slices came from:

Watch someone cutting up fruit or vegetables. Look at the shapes they make.

Sorting shopping

We're sorting shopping.

We've put away the things that go in the fridge or freezer!

We can sort out the rest in lots of different ways.

How have we sorted these things?

Big things and little things.

How have we sorted these things?

Can *you* explain how?

Can *you* sort some shopping? Find lots of ways of sorting it.

Then you can help put it away!

Teddy bags

I made a sleeping bag for my teddy.

I cut 2 big rectangles of paper.

 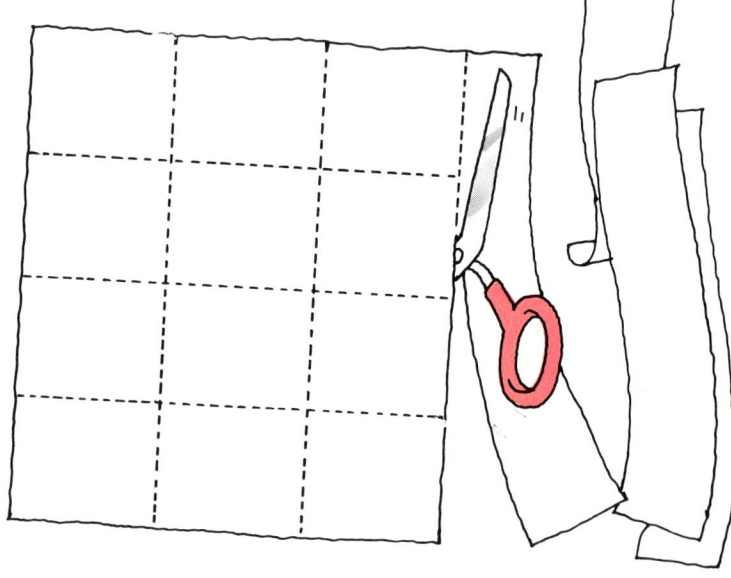

Then I drew patterns on them and coloured them in.

I like triangles!

I stapled the 2 bits together.
My Mum helped me.

Colour in these teddy bags.

I'm tired.
I want to
go to bed.

Could you make
a sleeping bag
for one of your
toys?

Dotty drawing

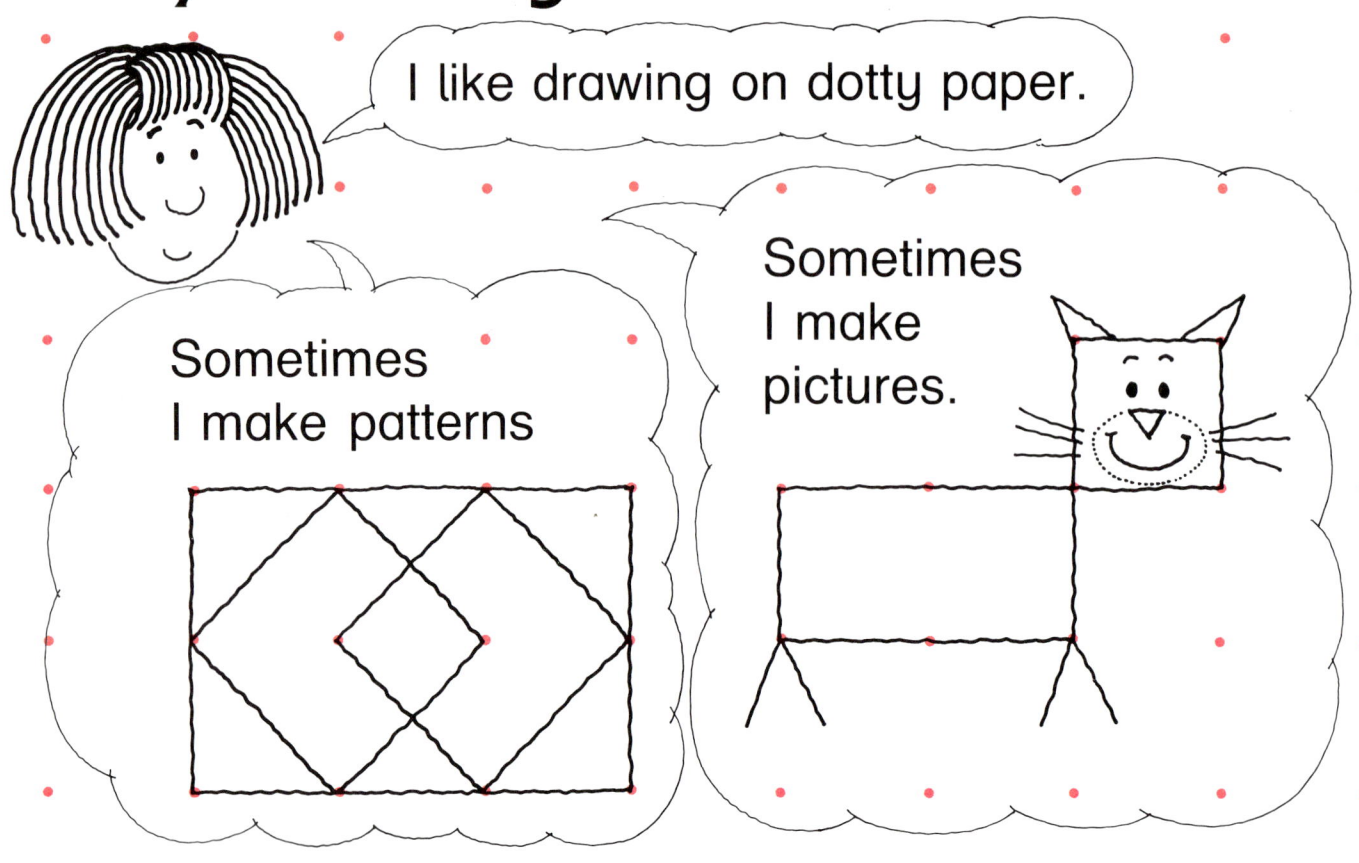

I like drawing on dotty paper.

Sometimes I make patterns

Sometimes I make pictures.

Draw some patterns and pictures.
You can colour them in, if you want to.

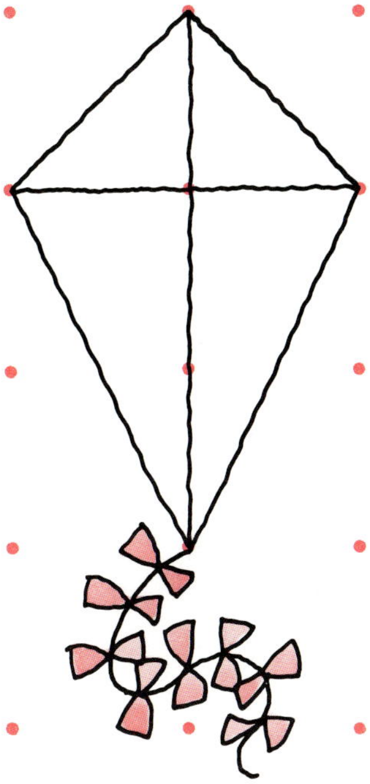

Mirror pictures

You need a mirror for this page.

Put the mirror on each picture to make the animal complete.

Put the mirror along the dotty line.

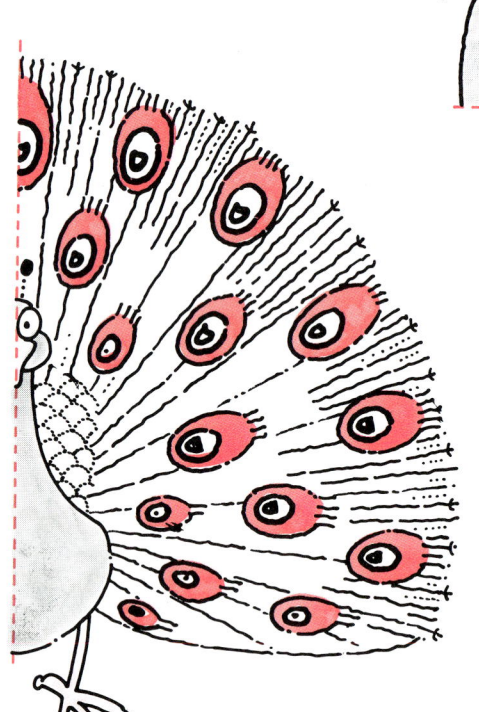 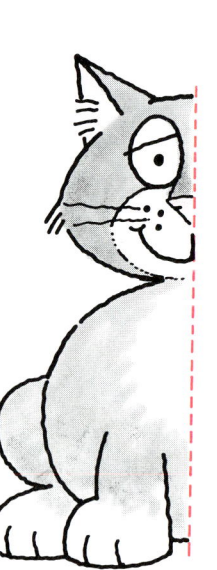 

Try drawing half of a picture yourself, and look at it with a mirror.